exerciseBALL

Fun, safe, and effective workouts with your Swiss Ball

exercise
BALL

Sara Rose

p

This is a Parragon Publishing Book
This edition published in 2006

Parragon Publishing
Queen Street House
4 Queen Street
Bath BA1 1HE, UK

ISBN: 1-40548-348-2

Printed in China

Created and produced by
THE BRIDGEWATER BOOK COMPANY

contents

Introduction

Get ready to roll your way to fitness with this revolutionary fitness tool! Whether you're a complete beginner, a regular gym-goer, or an elite athlete, working out with an exercise ball will give you a defined physique and a stronger, healthier, injury-free body.

Exercises that use a ball work on your body's muscle groups from a strong central core, using good breathing techniques, strong mental focus, and smooth, flowing movements throughout. It's an intelligent workout that combines the best elements of Western and Eastern exercise disciplines—muscle tone, strength, and intensity of movement with contemplation, relaxation techniques, and mind-body connections. It's an extremely safe, holistic, nonstressful, and effective way to work out and can be performed almost anywhere, any time, because the equipment is light, hardwearing, portable, and cheap. Working out with an exercise ball is also fun!

History

First made in 1963 by an Italian plastics manufacturer, the exercise ball became known otherwise as the "Swiss Ball" because American physiotherapists saw it used as a therapy tool in clinics in Switzerland. During the past two decades, they have become increasingly popular for personal training and home programs, and in exercise classes.

Key benefits

The whole point about using an exercise ball is that it is an unstable base, which makes you work extra muscles and develop new skills—the simple act of sitting on the ball improves postural strength and awareness. Your abdominal and spinal muscles, which act as a splint around your spine, will become stronger, and you'll also learn exercises to help strengthen and protect your back. Over time, your movements will become more fluid and graceful, and of course your fitness, strength, and stamina will all improve. As an added bonus, using a ball increases your

HOW TO USE THIS BOOK

This book will enable you to take control of your own fitness and decide when and where to exercise. However, it is not intended as a substitute for taking classes with an exercise ball instructor, who can help you to understand the principles and movements more fully. Read through all the introductory pages before trying the exercises so that you understand vital safety points and the fundamental elements of using a ball, which will help you to perform the exercises correctly. Don't try to do too many exercises at once. Practice several times a week if you can, building up the amount of time you spend and the types of exercises you do.

proprioception—your unconscious perception of the world around you—improving balance and fine-tuning motor (movement) skills. Ball-based exercise is also excellent for reducing stress—stretching encourages greater relaxation, particularly when combined with mental focus and a good breathing technique.

Nearly everyone can benefit from working out on an exercise ball, whatever their level of fitness. Even if you haven't exercised for years or have recently had a baby, you can start by doing a few stretches and bounces, and make your workout harder as your strength improves.

Caution

Always check with your doctor before starting a new exercise program. It's essential to take care when exercising during the first three months of pregnancy, as this is the time when there is the highest risk of miscarriage.

1 **Body** and **mind** basics

Exercising with a ball is one of the best ways there is to improve the way your body looks, feels, and works, because it gives both your mind and your body a good workout. Read this section to find out how it works on all aspects of your physique—your bones, muscles, ligaments, and joints. You'll find information on posture (the way you position yourself when sitting, standing, or lying down), which has a huge impact on your appearance and physical well-being, and tips on how to make sure your posture is as good as possible to keep your body in alignment and functioning efficiently.

By training your mind to exert a greater influence over your body, you can direct your energy toward what you want to achieve. This chapter explains the connections between mind and body, and shows how the power of positive thinking will make your exercise routine more effective. The following pages will also show you how to make your breathing most effective and how to ensure your movements are precise and controlled so that you get the most from your workout.

Body basics

The skeleton is your body's framework, made up of 206 bones that support the body and allow you to move. Bones are tough and rigid, but joints let bones bend and turn and muscles fixed to the bones permit an enormous range of movement. When joints, and muscles are not used regularly they lose strength and mobility, increasing the risk of injury or pain. Ball-based exercises work to align bone over bone and joint over joint, bringing your skeleton back into its correct position. The natural flow and motion of an exercise ball mobilizes, stretches, and relaxes your body, preventing joint stiffness and muscle tightness. This improves the way you move and reduces the risk of injury.

The spine

Your spine (backbone) is an S-shaped, flexible curve, comprising 33 bones (vertebrae) stacked on top of each other, which holds you upright and allows you to move in all directions. The vertebrae encase and protect the spinal cord, which carries messages between the brain and the spinal nerves, and have shock-absorbing discs between each one. The most important are the seven cervical vertebrae that support your neck; the 12 thoracic vertebrae anchoring the ribs and chest, protecting the lungs; and the five lumbar vertebrae holding up the back (these are particularly vulnerable to back pain and injury).

Muscles and movement

Muscles comprise millions of tiny protein filaments that contract and relax to produce movement. Most muscles are attached to bone

by tendons and are under the conscious control of your brain. Nerves transmit electrical signals from the brain, which cause the cells within the muscle to contract. Movement is caused by muscles pulling on tendons, which move the bones at the joints. Muscles work in pairs so that bones can move in two directions, and most movements involve the use of several muscle groups. Anterior muscles are in the front of the body, posterior muscles at the back. Many exercise programs focus on the anterior muscles, because these are the ones we see in the mirror, but this can increase the likelihood

TYPES OF MOVEMENT

You will come across the following terms in this book:

- Flexion **to bend a limb or the spine**

- Extension **which straightens a limb or the spine**

- Abduction **when you move away from the center of your body, for example, by raising your leg horizontally**

- Adduction **when you move toward the center of your body, for example, by lowering your arms to your sides**

- Rotation **when the body turns on its axis**

of poor posture and injury. This book works the anterior and posterior muscles to benefit your whole body.

Joints

A joint is the connection between two bones. Most joints move freely and are known as synovial joints. These include the fingers, wrists, elbows, shoulders, hips, knees, ankles, and toes. The best way of taking care of joints is to keep them fluid and flexible by exercising. Semi-movable joints, such as those in the spine and pelvis, are less flexible but give greater stability.

All about posture

Good posture happens when your spine is in natural alignment. It helps you stand and sit properly, reduces the strain on your back, and allows your internal organs to function efficiently. Posture also affects your appearance and the way others perceive you. When you are standing properly, you will look and feel more confident and elegant. If your posture is incorrect, every movement you make will be inefficient, leading to tiredness, weakness, aching muscles and joints, and an increased risk of injury.

What is good posture?

Good posture looks natural and relaxed, not slouched or hunched. When you are standing, your neck should be in line with your spine with your head balanced squarely on top, your shoulder blades set back and down and your spine long and naturally curving. Your hips should be straight. When sitting, you should sit up straight with your feet flat on the floor and your lower back supported.

How to check your posture

Stand in front of a full-length mirror to check your standing posture. Look to see if the following applies to you:

- Ear lobes level
- Shoulders level
- Equal distance between shoulders and ears
- Equal distance between arms and body
- Hips level
- Kneecaps level

Now, turn and look at yourself standing sideways. Imagine there is a straight line drawn down the center of your body. In an ideal posture, the line will pass through the center of the ear lobe, the tip of the shoulder, halfway through the chest, slightly behind the hip, and just outside the ankle bone.

Perfect posture

Standing straight with your body in perfect alignment is often easier said than done but the trick is to practice until it becomes second nature. Stand with your feet hip-width apart. Gently pull up through your legs, keeping your knees slightly bent. Lengthen your spine, contract your abdominal muscles, and stand tall. Keep your shoulders down and relaxed so that your neck is as long as possible, and make sure your weight is evenly distributed over both feet. To check you are doing this correctly, stand against a wall to practice. Place your hand between the wall and your lower back. You should just be able to place your fingers through the gap. If you can get your whole hand through, your back is too arched or your pelvis is tilted too far back. If you can't get your hand through at all, your back is too flat and your pelvis too far forward.

Mental focus

Using an exercise ball involves mental as well as physical exercise. The aim is to strengthen the connection between mind and body to bring about positive effects on your body, both internal and external. Learning to concentrate your mind and let go of bodily tension before you move are vital elements that help to make the practice of exercise ball techniques a complete mind-body experience.

To feel the full benefit of each exercise, you need to approach each one with good mental focus. By concentrating on how and where you are moving, you are more likely to move correctly and safely. Furthermore, you will become more expert at interpreting the way your body responds to each exercise. This will help you to judge more accurately the correct state of tension or relaxation that is required for a particular exercise.

The power of positive thinking

Using your mind and emotions will help you get the most from your workout. Use positive thoughts while you are exercising and focus on what you are doing right, rather than what you are getting wrong. Telling yourself that you are doing well can make you do even better, while sending negative messages to yourself sets you up to fail. To get yourself into the right frame of mind, use affirmations (making positive statements such as "My arm muscles are becoming more toned") and visualizations.

Take time to relax before exercising—this will help your body to release muscular tension.

Relaxation

When your body and mind are under stress your muscles become constricted, restricting the blood supply and dramatically affecting the way your body functions. One of the simplest ways of relaxing is to use a technique called "progressive muscle relaxation," which tenses and releases all the major muscle groups. Lie down, close your eyes, and concentrate on breathing slowly. Tense and release the muscles in each foot then loosen and relax it. Work your way up your body from your toes to your head, tensing and releasing each muscle group. Try this before you start your Swiss Ball exercises.

Creating mental pictures that correspond to what you are trying to do in your workout can be enormously useful in helping you to perform the exercise correctly. As you perform each exercise, think about how each part of your body feels and try to visualize these parts. It may take a bit of time to learn the techniques but it will be worth the effort.

BASIC VISUALIZATION

Using visualization helps you to evoke positive physical and psychological responses through your subconscious mind. Perform this simple visualization exercise to relax and calm your mind before you start your workout. Choose a quiet, comfortable place where you won't be disturbed. Sit or lie down and breathe slowly, trying to relax your body. Focus on your chosen mental image—for example, visualize somewhere beautiful outdoors, such as a mountain, park, garden, or empty beach—and picture yourself there. At the same time you can repeat positive affirmations such as "I am happy and relaxed." Maintain this image for about ten minutes, breathing slowly and rhythmically as you do so.

Stay in control

When you're using an exercise ball you need to be in control at all times. Along with focusing your mind, you need to learn how to use your breathing and how to make your movements coordinated, smooth, and flowing. Otherwise, you're liable to strain or injure yourself. Learning to move in a controlled way helps your body to reach its potential. With a little practice you'll be doing this automatically.

The importance of breathing properly

Breathing is something you do without thinking, but it can be consciously controlled. Correct breathing comes from the deepest area of the lungs, and benefits both your body and mind. But years of stress and poor lifestyle have left most of us with shallow, rapid breathing, whereby we use only the top third of our lungs.

Learn to breathe properly and you'll benefit from a lower heart-rate, reduced blood pressure, and lower levels of stress hormones. And breathing properly is essential when you're exercising—the rule is to breathe in through your nose just before you make a movement and breathe out through your mouth with each effort.

TAKE A DEEP BREATH

It can be quite hard to do this, but practice the following exercise, known as abdominal breathing, to learn how to breathe more deeply. Here the diaphragm, the sheet of muscle forming the top of the abdomen, is used to help the lungs inflate and deflate without effort. You may feel slightly dizzy at first—this is because you are taking in more oxygen than usual, which can make you feel light-headed.

- Lie on your back with your knees bent and your feet hip-width apart. Place your exercise ball on your chest.

- Roll the ball down to your stomach.

- Close your eyes and breathe in slowly through your nose.

- Hold the breath for a few seconds then breathe out slowly through your mouth.

- Notice that the ball gently rises and falls with your abdominal muscles.

- Repeat three or four times. Focus on your breathing as you do this rather than on anything else.

Controlling your movements

All exercises should be done slowly and in a meditative fashion. You have to concentrate on what you're doing, and think about how your body is responding to each exercise. If any action feels quick or jerky, or hurts, you're not doing it properly. Each movement should flow in a slow, gentle manner. This lets your muscles warm up and stretch naturally. It takes time to learn a more gentle approach to movement, but if you try to keep your body relaxed as you move, with practice your body will become used to performing the exercises naturally.

ONE VERTEBRA AT A TIME

One of the main principles of using an exercise ball is that you should roll up gradually so that you are lifting only one vertebra off the floor at a time, and the same applies when you roll back down again. This takes practice, and to start with you will have to concentrate hard to make sure you are doing it properly.

2

Getting started

It is not difficult to practice Swiss Ball at home, and this chapter shows you what you need to do before you get started. It's important that you read through this carefully because you will not have a teacher to help you ensure that you practice properly. Here you'll find out all about the equipment you will need, including information on balls and how to choose the one that's right for you. You'll find a host of safety tips, and precautions for ball care. There's information on creating the right environment so that you can exercise safely, what to wear, and when and where to exercise. Finally, you'll find out all about warming up. It's often tempting to save time by skipping a warm-up and going straight into the exercises, particularly if time is short, but here you'll find out why it's vital to warm up your muscles before exercising, and there's a series of exercises to help you warm up properly.

Equipment

The only equipment you need for your exercise ball workout is:

● the right sized ball.

● hand weights—make sure they are within your comfortable lifting range because the ball provides an unstable base, making weight-lifting much harder. You can use cans of beans or plastic bottles of water if you don't have weights. Small weights help you focus on breathing, posture, and technique without straining your body. Important: if you're pregnant, have back problems or are just starting out, do NOT use weights.

● ankle weights—the wrap-around type with adjustable weight levels is best.

● a mat or towel, or padded surface, to protect your spine and prevent bruising. It's worth buying a proper sports mat if you can.

Exercise balls are widely available from sports stores and are not expensive. There are many exercise balls on the market, varying in color, size, cost, and quality. Be sure to choose one that is burst-resistant and designed to take at least 660 lbs (300 kg) in weight (remember that the ball will have to take the combined weight of your body and the weights you may be using). Burst-resistant balls are much safer and stronger, and more likely to maintain their shape; and if you accidentally roll over a sharp object they will deflate gradually rather than explode. Cheaper balls are often shiny and slippery, making them less safe.

Choosing the right size of ball

When you are sitting on your ball, your knees and hips should be at an angle of 90 degrees or more. Using a ball that is too small or too large makes exercising awkward. The length of your arm from the shoulder to the fingertip is generally a good way to work out which is the right ball for you, but try one out in the store to make sure.

ARM LENGTH	BALL SIZE REQUIRED
22.5–26 inches (56–65 cm)	22 inches (55 cm)
26.5–32 inches (66–80 cm)	26 inches (65 cm)
32.5–36 inches (81–90 cm)	30 inches (75 cm)
36 inches (more than 90 cm)	34 inches (85 cm)

Precautions

Do not use the ball outside, and don't let your children or pets play with it.

Keep the ball away from direct heat and out of sunlight.

Do not exercise wearing sharp objects such as belts or buckles.

Inflate your ball according to the manufacturer's advice using a hand-operated pump so that it is firm, but not tight like a drum, with a little give. A slightly firmer ball makes it harder to stabilize and balance.

Staying safe

● Start every exercise near something you can hold on to—this is essential if your balance is less than perfect or if you are pregnant.
● Never attempt any exercise you think you can't manage.
● Stop if you feel sick, tired, or very out of breath.
● Keep long hair tied back.

Exercise area

Choose a safe, nonslip area to exercise on. Your surroundings should be free of furniture and clutter. Check the floor for sharp objects, which could hurt you or damage the exercise ball. If possible, try to exercise in front of a full-length mirror so that you can check what you are doing.

What to wear

Remove any jewelry and avoid wearing clothing that will restrict your movements. Also avoid baggy clothes, which can get caught under the ball. Choose clothes you can exercise in comfortably, such as a T-shirt worn with leggings or shorts—you'll find that cotton and natural fibers are cooler than manmade ones. Leave your feet bare, or wear trainers.

When to exercise

You can perform these exercises at any time, so choose the time that best suits you, whether it's a morning session to give you a burst of energy or an evening session to help you relax after a busy day. But do wait at least an hour after eating before exercising—longer if it was a big meal.

How many exercises?

To start with, aim to do each exercise five times, but remember that it is the quality of the movement that is important, not the quantity. Start gently and build up the number of exercises as you become fitter and more adept at exercising with a ball. Don't attempt to do too much too soon.

How long should you exercise for?

Aim to exercise with a ball three or four times a week. You'll feel the benefits even if you can only manage ten minutes at a time. As you become fitter and stronger you'll find that you can easily increase your workout intensity and time.

GOOD PRACTICE

● To make your exercises effective and safe, spend a little time doing the following before and after your session:

Before you start

● Drink at least 8½ cups of water a day to make sure you're well hydrated (but don't drink a large amount before exercising).

● Make sure your practice area is clear.

● Relax. Don't start the session if you are feeling tense. Try the exercises on pages 14–17 to help you let go of tension.

● Warm up properly.

After your session

● Don't just stop moving after you've finished your session—have a shower or go for a stroll to help you make the transition back to your normal activity.

● Don't go straight to bed if you're exercising in the evening.

Warm up properly

Make sure you're well hydrated

23

Neutral spine

Exercises on a ball require you to keep your spine in neutral. This means that you maintain the natural curve in your back (see perfect posture, pages 12–13), and avoid arching your back or pressing it so far down that you lose its natural curve. For the exercises in this book to work, it's essential that you learn how to hold your body in neutral alignment when you are lying on your back (supine), on your front (prone), and when you are sitting on the ball. These positions will make your exercises safe and effective.

Supine step 2

Prone step 1

Supine

1 Lie down on your exercise mat with your knees bent and feet flat on the floor.

2 Pull your navel (bellybutton) toward the floor to tighten your abdominal muscles. Press your fingers just above the pelvic bones to feel these muscles tighten.

3 Keep your back in contact with the floor—do not arch it. The trick is to just lie there, breathe in and out, and let your back relax into its own natural, neutral position.

Prone

1 Kneel with the ball under your abdomen. Roll forward until the ball is under your knees.

2 Set your abdominal muscles (see right) and tighten your buttock muscles.

3 Do not let your spine arch or sag—it's essential to keep your back straight.

4 Hold this position until you feel stable.

Sitting properly

1 Sit on the ball with your back straight and both feet placed on the floor, hip-width apart.

2 Set your abdominal muscles (see right).

3 Relax your shoulders and gently squeeze your shoulder blades together to stop them from becoming rounded. If you force your shoulders back and your lower back arches away from the ball, your shoulders are still too rounded.

4 Try to think of your head sitting naturally on your shoulders, neither pulling it forward nor pushing it back.

5 Keep your breathing slow and steady.

SETTING YOUR ABDOMINAL MUSCLES

When you work out on the ball you are constantly switching on your core muscles to keep your back and the ball still, so correct technique is vital. You have to set your abdominals in nearly every exercise, and practicing the setting action is a very important preliminary step.

Sit on the center of the ball and place one hand in the small of your back.

Now place your other hand on your lower abdomen, below your navel. The deep abdominals lie beneath this area. Lengthen your spine but relax your shoulders and your breathing.

Imagine a belt under your hands. Gently draw your front hand toward your back as though tightening the belt one notch.

This setting action should feel light and subtle. If you suck in your waist or hold your breath the action becomes ineffective as you won't be reaching the deep stabilizing muscles.

Warming up

You should always warm up to stretch your muscles, tendons, and ligaments before exercising, even if you are doing only a short session, otherwise you are likely to injure yourself. Warming up should involve a few minutes of aerobic exercise such as jogging on the spot followed by a series of stretches. Hold each stretch for a count of ten if you can, unless otherwise instructed. Read the following pages for ideas on how to do it, or you might like to think of your own exercises. Use the same stretches to cool down to loosen any muscles that feel cramped or tight. Remember to keep your back straight throughout your warm-up.

Reach and squat

1 Stand tall with your feet wide apart, holding the ball above your head.

2 Bend your knees and, keeping your back straight, bring the ball toward the floor.

3 Straighten your knees and reach up again.

4 Repeat three or four times.

Shoulder stretch

1 Kneel on your exercise mat with the ball in front of your head.

2 Place your forearms on the ball and let your body relax downward so that you can feel a gentle stretch in your shoulders.

3 Hold for a count of ten, release, and repeat three or four times.

Pec stretch

1 Kneel on the floor with the ball to your side and your hand outstretched on the ball.

2 Gently lower your chest toward the ground until you feel a stretch in the front of your chest and shoulder. Keep your back straight as you stretch.

3 Hold for a count of ten, release, and repeat three or four times, then do the exercise on the other side of your body.

Hip stretch

1   Sit sidesaddle on the ball, with your right foot forward and your left foot back, resting on the toe. Your hips should be level and facing forward.

2   Drop down and gently push your right hip forward until you feel a stretch,

3   Repeat using the other leg.

Spine stretch

1   Kneel before your ball and roll forward so that the ball is under your body between your hips and chest, hands on the floor in front of you.

2   Let your body mold itself over the ball and relax in this position for a count of 30 or longer. You might like to rock gently back and forward.

Inner thigh stretch

1   Sit on your ball with your feet slightly more than hip-width apart. Rest your hands on your thighs.

2   Stretch one leg out to the side until you feel a pull on the inside of the thigh.

3   Hold for a count of ten, release, and repeat using the other leg.

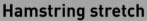

Hamstring stretch

1 Sit on the ball with your legs stretched out
   in front of you, hip-width apart and your
   hands resting just above your knees.
   Keep your spine straight and tighten your
   abdominal muscles.

2 Bending from the hips, slowly reach
   forward until you feel a stretch in
   the back of your thigh.

3 Hold for a count of ten, release, and repeat
   three or four times.

Quad stretch

1 Stand with the ball behind you.

2 Bend your left knee behind you and rest
   your shin on the ball.

3 Keeping your back straight, bend your right
   leg forward until you can feel a stretch in
   the front of the thigh on the ball.

4 Hold for a count of ten, release, and repeat
   three or four times. Repeat the exercise on
   the other leg.

3 Stability

The muscles between your ribs and hips, the back and abdominal muscles, form a corset that stabilizes, supports, and protects your spine. These core muscles are hard to find—generally, you can't feel them or see them working—but with time and practice you will become more aware of these stabilizing muscles and notice the difference they make to exercise and daily life. This chapter contains a series of exercises designed to train your core muscles to work most effectively to protect your back from injury and to improve your posture and breathing. Working on your core stability will make all your movements more precise and stable. It will also improve your balance and proprioceptive awareness—the unconscious coordination between your mind and body. Before beginning this section, you must be able to find your body's neutral alignment naturally—practice the exercises on pages 24–25.

Sitting balance ● beginners

Sitting on the ball and lifting your feet from the floor is a great way to train your core stabilizing muscles.

1 Sit on the ball with your feet hip-width apart.

2 Lift one foot off the floor and hold for a count of five.

3 Put the foot down, then lift the other foot.

3

Look out

If you lift your feet too high you will wobble on the ball and lose your postural alignment.

2

The bridge

The bridge is used as the starting position in many exercises, so it's important to be able to do this one properly. It works the abdominal muscles, lower back, pelvic stabilizers, gluteals, and hamstrings. When exercising, always keep your spine in neutral and do not let your back arch. Keep the ball as still as possible throughout.

Basic bridge ● beginners

1 Lie on your back with your arms by your sides. Place your feet on the ball so that it is resting under your calf muscles. Tighten your abdominal muscles.

2 Lift your hips off the floor using your buttock muscles, until your body is diagonal from shoulders to knees.

Bridge with leg lifts ● beginners

Lifting one leg from the ball strengthens the muscles at the back of the buttocks and thighs while increasing balance and control in the stabilizing muscle groups.

1 Lie on your back with your arms by your sides. Place your feet on the ball so that the ball is resting under your calf muscles. Tighten your abdominal muscles.

2 Lift your hips off the floor using your buttock muscles, until your body is diagonal from shoulders to knees.

3 Slowly raise one leg from the ball and hold for a count of five.

4 Return to the ball and repeat using the other leg.

High bridge ● intermediate

1 Lie on your back with your arms by your
sides and your knees bent. Place your feet
on top of the ball.

2 Tighten your abdominal muscles and slowly
lift your hips from the floor using your
buttock muscles, keeping your knees bent
and feet on the ball until your body is
diagonal from knees to shoulders.

3 Hold for a count of five, then return to
the start position and repeat.

Bridge with hand weights ● advanced

This trains the brain and muscles to maintain stability while carrying out another task.

2

1 Lie on your back with your arms stretched out. Place your feet on the ball so that it is resting under your calf muscles. Tighten your abdominal muscles.

2 Lift your hips off the floor using your buttock muscles, until your body is diagonal from shoulders to knees.

3 Bring the weights out in front of you at chest level, keeping the ball as still as possible. Hold for a count of five, lower arms, and repeat.

Caution

Do not do these exercises if you have lower back pain.

3

Reverse bridge

Again, this is the starting point for many exercises and you need to be able to perform it correctly to work out safely. It works the abdominal muscles, lower back, pelvic stabilizers, gluteals, and hamstrings while improving your balance. Keep your spine in neutral throughout and do not let your back sag or arch. Keep the ball as still as possible.

Look out

If your head is hanging back over the ball, walk farther forward. If your chin is on your chest, walk back a little.

Rolling in and out of reverse bridge
● beginners to intermediate

1 Sit on the ball with your hands by your sides and your feet hip-width apart.

2 To move into reverse bridge, walk your feet forward, rolling your hips down, and lying back on the ball as you do so. Stop when your shoulder blades are on the ball. Your knees should be bent at a 90-degree angle, and your abdominal muscles tight.

3 Lower your head to the ball and lift your hips.

4 Hold for a count of five. To make this harder, bring your feet together.

5 Drop your hips again and lift your head off the ball.

6 Slowly walk your feet back, pressing your lower back into the ball as you go, and return to the starting position.

3

Reverse bridge with leg extension
● beginners to intermediate

1 Lie with the ball under your shoulders and your feet hip-width apart in the reverse bridge position.

2 Tighten your abdominal muscles and lift one leg away from the floor, keeping your knee bent.

3 Hold for a count of five, then return to the starting position.

4 Repeat using the other leg.

Side walk ● intermediate

1 Lie with the ball beneath your shoulders in the reverse bridge position. Keep your feet hip-width apart and tighten your abdominal muscles.

2 Hold your arms out horizontally to the sides. Slowly walk sideways so that the ball passes from under one shoulder to under the other. Do this exercise at least once from side to side and build up to repeating the movement several times.

Reverse bridge with hip dips ● intermediate

1 Lie back on the ball with your head and shoulders supported and your feet hip-width apart in the reverse bridge position.

2 Place your hands wherever is comfortable—under your head, resting on your hips, or down by your sides.

3 Tighten your abdominal muscles and lower your buttocks toward the floor.

4 Press through your heels and contract your buttock muscles to raise your hips back up to the horizontal position.

4

Abdominals

The previous chapter worked on your abdominal muscles in their stabilizing capacity, but the exercises in this section go further by concentrating on strengthening and toning them, which will improve your breathing, spinal strength, and posture. There are four abdominal muscle groups, forming a natural corset around your middle. They support your lower spine, protect your internal organs, and let you twist, bend, and sit up. The transversus abdominis, the deepest of the abdominal muscles, wraps horizontally around your waist and keeps your lower spine stable by narrowing the abdominal wall. The rectus abdominis runs up from the pubic bone to the bottom of the ribcage. It lets your trunk bend because it pulls your ribs toward the pelvis, and is important for maintaining posture. The external and internal obliques, running up the sides of your torso, let you bend to the side and twist your spine.

Basic abdominal exercises

The exercises on the following pages focus on giving a good workout to the transversus abdominis, which is below your navel, and the rectus abdominis. These are sometimes known as your lower abdominal muscles, but because all your abdominal muscles are attached to the pelvis, it's not really correct to call them this. These muscles support and strengthen your lower spine as well as playing an important part in keeping your pelvis stable. In addition to strengthening the abdominal muscles, the exercises will teach you how to curl your upper body while keeping your spine in alignment. Try to keep your pelvis in neutral and do not pull up your tailbone.

Preparation for abdominals ● beginners

This will prepare you for the more difficult abdominal exercises.

1 Place the ball against a wall.

2 Lie on the floor with your feet on the ball and your knees bent. Place a folded towel or small cushion between your thighs.

3 Very gently, breathe in through your nose. As you breathe out, feel your stomach muscles pulling down to the floor.

4 Hold for a count of four. Squeeze the towel or cushion with your thighs. This will contract your deep internal muscles.

2

4

Basic abdominals ● beginners

1 Lie on the floor with your feet on the ball, with your knees bent and legs together.

2 Place your hands on your hip bones to stabilize your pelvis.

3 Very gently, breathe in and let your knees fall open to hip-width apart.

4 As you breathe out, bring your legs back together, pulling your stomach in so that your navel is being drawn down and into your spine.

4

3

Abdominals
● beginners to intermediate

1 Sit on the ball with feet hip-width apart.

2 Lean backward, moving the ball forward with your pelvis. Stretch your arms out in front of you to keep your balance.

3 When you feel the lower abdominal muscles tighten, hold for a count of five then return to a seated position by pulling in the pelvis.

4 To make the exercise harder, try holding the position for longer periods. You could also cross your arms over your chest.

Basic crunches ● beginners

Putting your feet on the ball increases the stabilizing ability of your abdominal muscles. It also makes your abdominal muscles work a little harder than in the previous exercise.

2 Tighten your abdominal muscles and breathe steadily.

3 Begin to nod your chin while your head is still on the floor.

4 Lift your head, bending the upper body, and raising your arms parallel to the floor. Use your abdominal muscles, not your hands, to lift your head.

5 Hold for a count of four. You should be looking at your thighs, not at the ceiling.

6 Return your head and arms to the floor.

1 Lie on your back with both heels resting on the ball, your hips and knees at an angle and your arms resting on the floor.

Crunches ● intermediate

1 Lie on your back.

2 Grasp the ball under your knees and lift it from the floor.

3 Tighten your abdominal muscles and put your hands either side of your head.

4 Slowly lift your shoulders from the floor toward your knees.

5 Hold for a count of five and roll your shoulders back down to the start position.

Take care

HEAD POSITION
When lying on your back you need to make sure your head is not tilted, making your neck arch. Drop your chin gently forward instead.

1

Crunches ● advanced

1 Lie on your back. Grasp the ball underneath your calves and lift them from the floor to an angle of about 45 degrees.

2 Tighten your abdominal muscles and put your hands either side of your head.

3 Hold this position, and slowly lift your shoulders from the floor toward your knees.

4 Hold for a count of five then roll your shoulders back down to the floor, keeping your legs raised.

3

Obliques

These exercises work the obliques, the crisscrossing abdominal muscles that we don't use as much as the others. These muscles let you bend from side to side and rotate the trunk.

Side crunch ● beginners

1 Lie on one side with the ball beneath you and your feet placed against a wall, one in front of the other.

2 Cross your arms over your chest.

3 Slowly lift your upper torso from the ball and hold for a count of five.

4 Return to the starting position.

5 Repeat the exercise with the ball beneath you on the other side.

1

3

Sitting obliques
● intermediate to advanced

1 Sit on the ball and roll forward with your pelvis until the ball is under your lower spine.

2 Put your hands either side of your head.

3 Lift your upper torso toward your knees and over to the right side. At the same time, lift your right leg toward the left shoulder, bending the knee.

4 Hold for a count of five then return to the starting position.

5 Repeat on the other side.

6 To make this harder, use ankle weights.

3

6

5

Spinal strength and mobility

The spine is a complex structure that works hard to enable us to go about our daily lives. Most back pain is the result of a combination of poor posture, instability, and the activities of daily life gradually weakening your spine. These exercises are designed to improve spinal strength and mobility to strengthen your back against injury. The main muscles worked in this section are the trapezius, a long, diamond-shaped muscle connected to the neck and upper and middle back; the latissimus dorsi, a large muscle that wraps around the torso until it reaches the upper arm; and the erector spinae, bands of muscles that run parallel to your spine (these work constantly to keep the spine upright and take turns contracting so that their action is constant over long periods of time). Muscles in your legs, shoulders, arms, and stomach will also benefit from these exercises. Make sure you keep your spine aligned throughout.

Spinal strength

These exercises work on strengthening the deep stabilizing muscles around your shoulders, pelvis, and spine to improve spinal strength and enable you to lengthen your spine. Make sure you work at a distance from the ball where you can maintain good movement control and keep your spine in neutral. If your back is arching or sagging, step your hands backward to shorten the distance between you and the ball.

2

Basic plank ● beginners

1   Kneel on the floor with the ball in front of you.

2   Bend your elbows and place your forearms on the ball.

3   Tighten your abdominal muscles and slowly push off from your feet and knees so that the ball rolls away from your body.

4   Hold for a count of five then return to the start position.

3

Plank ● intermediate

1 Kneel on the floor with your elbows bent and resting on the ball.

2 Tighten your abdominal muscles and slowly push forward with your feet.

3 Let the ball roll away from your body and extend your legs as far as possible, keeping your elbows bent.

4 Hold the position for a count of five and slowly return to the start position.

Plank with leg raises ● advanced

1 Kneel on the floor with your elbows bent and resting on the ball.

2 Tighten your abdominal muscles and slowly push forward with your feet. Let the ball roll away from your body, keeping your arms bent at the elbows.

3 Slowly raise one leg from the floor.

4 Hold for a count of five then slowly lower to the start position.

5 Repeat using the other leg.

Look out

Ensure that your shoulders, hips, and feet are in a straight line.

The swan ● beginners

1. Lie with the ball under your stomach and pelvis and your hands on the floor, shoulder-width apart.

2. Plant your toes on the floor and keep your legs straight, hip-width apart.

3. Lift your head so that there is a long line from your head to the toes.

4. Tighten your abdominal muscles and slowly push your pelvis into the ball as you look up and extend your spine away from the ball.

5. Hold for a count of five then return to the start position.

Swan dive

● intermediate to advanced

1 Place your mat next to the wall. Lie with the ball under your stomach and pelvis and your hands on the ball, shoulder-width apart.

2 Plant the balls of your feet against the wall and keep your legs straight, hip-width apart.

3 Lift your head so that there is a long line from your head to the toes.

4 Reach your arms out in front of you.

5 Hold for a count of five then return to the start position.

Take care

These exercises are hard work for your back. Take frequent rests, and if an exercise causes you pain stop doing it immediately.

Spinal mobility

Poor posture—caused, for example, by spending long periods of time hunched over a computer—compresses the backbones, causing pain and misalignment. These exercises will release your back and stretch out your shoulders to increase spinal mobility so that you can avoid back strain. Note that there are no advanced exercises included in this section.

Cat stretch ● beginners

1 Rest your palms on the ball and kneel as far away as you can. For extra stability, support the ball against a wall.

2 Curl your chin into your chest, pull your stomach into your spine, and stretch out your lower back, pulling your abdominal muscles in as you do so.

3 Hold for a count of five, then press your chest down and gently lengthen your neck and head.

Hip circles ● beginners

1 Sit on the ball with your feet shoulder-width apart and your hands touching the ball on either side.

2 Tighten your abdominal muscles and use your pelvis to rotate the ball slowly three times to the right in small clockwise circles.

3 Repeat on the other side.

Look out

If you feel your neck crunching, you've taken it too far back.

Back extension ● intermediate

1 Sit on the ball with your feet hip-width apart and your hands on your thighs.

2 Slowly walk your feet forward until the ball is under your back.

3 Let your spine arch backward and relax over the ball.

4 Take your arms overhead and push into the feet to arch the body over the ball.

5 Drop your pelvis to the floor and roll off the ball to get out of this position safely.

Back extension ● beginners

1 Sit on the ball with your feet hip-width apart and your hands on your thighs.

2 Slowly walk your feet forward until the ball is under your back.

3 Let your spine arch backward and relax over the ball, and rock gently to and fro for a count of ten.

4 Drop your pelvis to the floor and roll off the ball to get out of this position safely.

2

Spinal rotation ● intermediate

1   Lie on your back with your knees bent.

2   Hold the ball on the floor behind your head.

3   Roll your knees to the left side and the ball to the right. Hold the stretch for a count of ten.

4   Keep your feet resting on the floor as you slowly roll to the other side.

5

Lower body

6

This chapter contains a series of exercises designed to work the leg, hip, and buttock muscles to increase strength, coordination, flexibility, and stability. This should reduce the risk of injury when you are playing sport, enabling you to concentrate on improving your skills. When muscles are too tight in your legs and hips it can result in back problems and pain, and these exercises will improve your posture to reduce these effects. They will also help to tone your bottom and thighs, giving you a longer, leaner look. Using the exercise ball, which is an unstable base, brings several other important muscles into play, such as the deep abdominals, as well as the target muscle group. You should feel your abdominal muscles working in all the leg exercises, and, of course, you need to keep your spine in neutral throughout. Once again, strength and core stability unite to create an efficient and powerful mode of exercising.

Basic movements

These exercises help to tone and stretch your legs and act as a gentle warm-up for more difficult exercises. They also promote strength and mobility in your spine and stabilizing pelvic muscles. Adding arm to leg movements challenges your balance and coordination. Tighten your abdominal muscles throughout.

Toe taps ● beginners

1 Sit on the ball with your feet hip-width apart and flat on the floor, your arms hanging loosely by your sides.

2 Stretching out one leg, tap the toes of one foot on the floor in front of you ten times.

3 Return to the starting position and repeat on the other side.

2

Foot kicks ● intermediate to advanced

1 Sit on the ball with your feet slightly wider than hip-width apart and flat on the floor and your arms hanging loosely by your sides.

2 Hold your arms out at chest level to help you balance. Tighten your abdominal muscles and keep your back straight.

3 Kick your right foot up until the knee is as straight as possible.

4 Return the foot to the floor and repeat with the left leg.

5 Repeat the whole exercise, but this time, when kicking up a leg, swing the opposite arm upward.

6 To make this exercise more difficult, use ankle weights.

Look out

If you lift your feet too high you will lose your balance.

3

5

6

Leg lifts and inner thigh lifts

These exercises make your deep stabilizing muscles work to control the weight and movements of your legs. They also strengthen the inner thigh muscles and those that control side bending of the lower spine.

Frog ● beginners

1 Lie on your back with the soles of your feet together and resting on the ball.

2 Let your knees fall open to the side so they resemble frogs' legs.

3 Rest your hands on your inner thighs. Relax.

4 Hold this position for as long as is comfortable.

Bend and stretch

● intermediate to advanced

1 Lie on your back with your knees bent.

2 Pick up the ball between your ankles and squeeze together, pulling your knees toward you.

3 Sit up far enough to rest your upper body on your elbows.

4 Straighten your legs out diagonally and hold for a count of five.

5 Return to the starting position.

Hip exercises

These exercises focus on working the hip muscles, which play a very important part in stabilizing your pelvis and supporting your lower back, as well as keeping the hip joints flexible. Make sure you keep your spine in neutral alignment throughout the exercise.

Hip flexions ● beginners

1 Lie with the ball under your stomach.

2 Keeping yourself supported on your straightened arms, roll forward until the ball is under your shins.

3 Tighten your abdominal muscles and keep your spine straight. Then slowly bring your knees toward your chest, rolling the ball forward with you.

4 Hold for a count of three then stretch out your legs to return to the starting position.

2

2

Hip extensions ● beginners

1 Kneel on the floor with the ball under your stomach.

2 Tighten your abdominal muscles and slowly extend your left leg and right arm until they are horizontal. Keep your toes pointing toward the floor.

3 Hold for a count of five and return to the starting position.

4 Repeat using the other leg and arm.

Hip extensions ● advanced

1 Put on ankle weights and lie prone on the ball so that it is under your pelvis and stomach.

2 Lift your left leg, bend the knee, and push your foot up toward the ceiling. This should lift your thigh away from the ball.

3 Hold for a count of five then slowly return to the starting position.

4 Repeat on the other side.

Buttocks (gluteals)

The following exercises will tone and stretch your buttock muscles. Buttock muscles are not just for sitting on—they also help move your legs. Tension in the gluteals can lead to back problems and poor posture so it's very important to keep these muscles flexible and strong.

Gluteal stretch ● beginners

1 Lie on your back with your legs bent and your right heel resting on the ball.

2 Cross your left ankle over your right thigh and let your left knee fall outward.

3 Tighten your abdominal muscles and, using your right foot, roll the ball toward you until you feel a stretch behind your hip in your buttock.

4 Hold for a count of ten then return to the starting position.

5 Repeat using the other leg.

Basic bottom toner ● beginners

1 Lie on your front with the ball between your ribs and your hips. Your arms should be shoulder-width apart with the palms of your hands planted on the floor. Your toes should be touching the floor with your feet flexed for balance.

2 Slowly lift your left leg until it is pointing out straight behind you, keeping the buttock muscles clenched as you do so.

3 Hold for a count of five.

4 Return to the starting position and repeat with the other leg.

Bottom toner ● intermediate

1 Lie on your front with the ball between your ribs and your hips. Your arms should be shoulder-width apart with the palms of your hands planted on the floor. Your toes should be touching the floor with your feet flexed for balance.

2 Slowly lift both legs up, keeping your buttock muscles clenched as you do so.

3 Hold for a count of five then return to the starting position.

Hamstrings and quadriceps

These exercises work the hamstrings (back of the thigh) and quadriceps (front of the thigh). Strength, coordination, and stability are essential in these muscles if you are going to be able to walk, run, and play sports effectively. Tight quadriceps and hamstrings cause lower back pain and poor posture.

Look out

Your bottom should stay on the floor throughout.

Hamstring stretch ● beginners

1 Lie on your back with a towel or cushion beneath your head.

2 Rest your feet on the ball supported against a wall.

3 Roll the ball toward you, bending your knees until they are directly above your hips.

4 Hold one leg behind the thigh and extend it toward the ceiling.

5 Hold for a count of 15.

6 Bring the leg toward you, moving your hand up to your calf.

7 Return to the starting position and repeat on the other side.

3   4   6

Squat ● beginners to advanced

1 Don't use a mat for this exercise because of the risk of slipping. Stand with the ball between your lower back and the wall, and your feet hip-width apart. Rest your hands on your thighs and tighten your abdominal muscles.

2 Roll down to a seated squat position until your thighs are horizontal.

3 Hold for a count of five then slowly stand up.

4 To make this more difficult, hold weights by your side to further load the quadriceps.

7

Upper body

This chapter contains a series of exercises to improve flexibility, strength, and coordination in your shoulder and arm joints and to give you muscle definition in your chest, arms, and shoulders. Sitting on an unstable base stimulates activity in the deep back and abdominal muscles, and standing on your feet, pressing the ball against a wall, or using the ball as a bench are comfortable and efficient ways to train your body as a unit rather than just bulking up specific muscles. Adding light weights further tests your ability to keep your spine straight and strong, so you are strengthening your core while toning your upper body. Using weights also helps to stabilize the muscles in their joints, and helps you maintain strong bones and muscles as you age. Remember to keep your abdominal muscles pulled in as you exercise, and keep your spine in neutral throughout.

Press-ups and push ups

Using the ball means that all your body's muscles are worked to maintain balance and keep the spine in neutral, rather than just the shoulder and arm muscles. Make sure you work at a distance from the ball where you can maintain good control and spinal position. If your upper back is arching or your lower back swaying, step your hands back to shorten the distance between you and the ball.

Basic press-ups
● beginners to intermediate

1 Kneel with your hands on the ball.

2 Slowly walk the ball forward on your hands.

3 Tighten your abdominal muscles to keep your back straight and well supported.

4 Bend your elbows, slowly lowering your chest toward the ball. Do not lock your elbows.

5 Slowly push back up.

Wall push-up
● beginners to advanced

1 Stand holding the ball at chest height between you and the wall.

2 Roll the ball up to shoulder height.

3 Holding the ball against the wall, step back and keep your feet hip-width apart. Keep your body in a straight line from your shoulders to your heels.

4 Slowly bend your elbows outward to move your chest toward the wall.

5 Hold for a count of two then press back away from the wall to straighten your arms.

6 To make this harder, press up with one hand only, placing the other behind your back.

Caution

Do not do these exercises if you have a shoulder, neck or back problem.

Biceps and triceps

These exercises work the biceps, the muscles in the front of the upper arm that enable the elbow to bend and the forearm and hand to move toward the shoulder; and the triceps, in the back of the arm, which work to straighten the elbow. Try to keep your body steady and perform the exercises without moving your head.

Biceps curls
● beginners to advanced

1 Sit on the center of the ball with your legs just wider than hip-width apart.

2 Hold a weight in each hand by your sides with your palms facing inward.

3 Turn your forearms so that the palms face forward.

4 Tighten your abdominal muscles, then slowly bend one weight upward to shoulder level and pause for a count of two.

5 Slowly lower to waist level and repeat with the other arm.

6 To make this exercise more difficult, use heavier weights.

Triceps press
● beginners to intermediate

1 Sit on the center of the ball with your legs just wider than hip-width apart.

2 Hold one weight in both hands behind your head. Keep your elbows close to your forehead.

3 Slowly straighten your elbows to press the weight to the ceiling and hold for a count of two.

4 Slowly bend your elbows to lower the weight behind your head.

5 To make this exercise more difficult, use heavier weights.

Shoulders

It is important to stretch out your shoulders after performing the upper body strengthening exercises on the previous pages. These exercises work the levator scapulae at the back and sides of the neck, which lift the shoulders, and will improve flexibility in your shoulder joints and release tension in your chest muscles.

Double shoulder stretch ● all levels

1 Stand with the ball at chest height between you and the wall. Your hands should be on the ball and your arms slightly bent. Keep feet hip-width apart.

2 Tighten your abdominal muscles and keep your spine aligned.

3 Push the ball up the wall until your biceps are level with your ears. Hold for a count of five then return to the starting position.

Look out

If you are too close to the wall you will not feel the stretch. If you are too far away from the wall your back will arch and your heels will come off the ground.

1

3

1

2

Shoulder press
● intermediate to advanced

1 Sit on the ball with your feet hip-width
apart. Keep your arms bent with your
elbows at shoulder level, holding small
weights.

2 Tighten your abdominal muscles. Slowly
press the weights upward and toward each
other until they are touching, with your
arms fully extended.

3 Slowly lower the weights to the starting
position, bringing your elbows slightly
backward and drawing your shoulder
blades together.

4 To make this harder, raise alternate legs
as you press the weights.

4

Chest

This exercise works on the pectorals—
the chest muscles—and will also benefit
the upper back, midback, and
arm muscles.

2

Chest press ● all levels

1 Lie in the reverse bridge position with your head and neck supported by the ball. Tighten your abdominal muscles.

2 Start with the weights held just above your shoulders.

3 Slowly raise your arms, keeping your shoulder blades in contact with the ball.

4 Hold for a count of five, then return to the starting position.

5 Do single-arm raises for an extra challenge to pelvic and spinal stablity.

8

Workouts

The exercises in the workouts are photographic programs
for you to follow, but you can combine any of the exercises in
the book to create your own program. Each workout is a
complete session in itself, but you don't have to do all the
exercises if you don't want to. Remember to engage your mind
and control your body with precise movements as you work
out—it's the quality of movement that counts, rather than the
number of times you perform each exercise. The more you
practice, the easier you will find working out with an
exercise ball. Each program is designed to last for about
20 minutes, but can be made longer by increasing the
number of times you do each exercise. Perform three
or four times a week for optimum benefits. Always
start with the warming up exercises on pages 26–31
and stretch to cool down afterward. And remember to
check with your doctor before starting an exercise
program if you're new to exercising.

Beginners

This workout is ideal if you are just starting out or are looking for a light session. Make sure you warm up properly following the exercises on pages 26–31 before you begin, and stretch when you have finished.

Sitting positions

Sitting balance (page 34)

Toe taps (page 66)

Hip circles (page 61)

Lying on the floor

Basic abdominals (page 47)

Hamstring stretch (page 74)

Gluteal stretch (page 72)

Forward on the ball

Cat stretch (page 60)

The swan (page 58)

Basic bottom toner (page 73)

Basic plank (page 56)

Back on the ball

Rolling in and out of reverse bridge (page 39)

Back extension (beginners) (page 62)

Standing with the ball

Double shoulder stretch (page 82)

Wall push-up (page 79)

Squat (page 75)

MAKING THE MOST OF YOUR WORKOUT

Make sure you are relaxed before you begin.

Concentrate: think about how your body feels as you move, and what you are trying to achieve.

Pull in your stomach muscles so that you work from a strong core.

Keep your spine aligned.

Breathe in as you move into position and breathe out with each effort.

Move slowly and gracefully.

Intermediate

This is a slightly more challenging workout designed for those who are experienced in ball-based exercises. Make sure you warm up properly following the exercises on pages 26–31 before you begin, and stretch when you have finished.

Sitting positions

Sitting obliques (page 53)

Biceps curls (page 80)

Triceps press (page 81)

Lying on the floor

High bridge (page 37)

Intermediate crunches (page 50)

Spinal rotation (page 63)

Forward on the ball

Back on the ball

Standing with the ball

MAKING THE MOST OF YOUR WORKOUT

Make sure you are relaxed before you begin.

Concentrate: think about how your body feels as you move, and what you are trying to achieve.

Pull in your stomach muscles so that you work from a strong core.

Keep your spine aligned.

Breathe in as you move into position and breathe out with each effort.

Move slowly and gracefully.

Advanced

This is a tough workout for the very fit and experienced. Make sure you warm up properly following the exercises on pages 26–31 before you begin, and stretch when you have finished.

Sitting positions

Foot kicks (page 67)

Sitting obliques (page 53)

Shoulder press (page 83)

Lying on the floor

Crunches (advanced) (page 51)

Spinal rotation (page 63)

Bend and stretch (page 69)

Forward on the ball

Advanced hip extensions (page 71)
Swan dive (page 59)
Plank with leg raises (page 57)

Back on the ball

Chest press (page 85)
Reverse bridge with hip dips (page 42)

Standing with the ball

Double shoulder stretch (page 82)
Wall push-up (page 79)
Squat (page 75)

MAKING THE MOST OF YOUR WORKOUT

Make sure you are relaxed before you begin.

Concentrate: think about how your body feels as you move, and what you are trying to achieve.

Pull in your stomach muscles so that you work from a strong core.

Keep your spine aligned.

Breathe in as you move into position and breathe out with each effort.

Move slowly and gracefully.

Exercises during pregnancy and after

These gentle exercises will help you to maintain good posture and suppleness during pregnancy. Afterward, they will enable you to get your body back into shape after the birth, when the emphasis is on strengthening the deep abdominal muscles and the pelvic floor.

The exercises have been selected for their low impact, and for the support that they provide for the body's changed center of gravity during pregnancy. They should be performed without weights.

If you are pregnant, you must consult your doctor before following any exercise program. Make sure you warm up properly following the exercises on pages 26–31 before you begin and stretch when you have finished. If any exercise causes discomfort, stop and seek medical advice.

AN EXERCISE SPECIFICALLY FOR PREGNANCY

Bouncing on the ball

Sit on the center of the ball with both feet on the floor, hip-width apart.

Keep your spine aligned and your hands resting lightly on the top of the ball.

Extremely gently, bounce on the ball for up to 3 minutes.

MAKING THE MOST OF YOUR WORKOUT

Don't do any sit-ups or press-ups when pregnant, and always be particularly careful if exercising during the first three months of pregnancy, as this is the time when miscarriage is most likely.

You cannot pull in your stomach muscles when you are pregnant—instead, concentrate on your deep pelvic floor muscles, between the point of your pubic bone and your anus.

Look out

Keep your back as straight as possible in the sitting positions.

Sitting positions

Toe taps (*page 66*)
Hip circles (*page 61*)
Biceps curls (NO WEIGHTS) (*page 80*)
Triceps press (NO WEIGHTS) (*page 81*)

Lying on the floor

Hamstring stretch (*page 74*)
Gluteal stretch (*page 72*)

Forward on the ball

Cat stretch (*page 60*)

Standing with the ball

Double shoulder stretch (*page 82*)
Wall push-up (*page 79*)

Index

Acknowledgments

Exercise photography:

Ian Parsons

The publisher would like to thank:

Gemma Wright, Zoe Hall